*Journal*

PETER PAUPER PRESS, INC.
WHITE PLAINS, NEW YORK

The text in this journal is excerpted from *The Key to Life*, by Sophia Bedford-Pierce,
copyright © 1995 Peter Pauper Press, Inc.; *Believe in Yourself: A Woman's Journey*,
by Beth Mende Conny, copyright © 1996, 1998 Peter Pauper Press, Inc.; and
*Believe in Yourself*, by Beth Mende Conny, copyright © 2001, Peter Pauper Press, Inc.

Cover illustration by Lauren Wan

Copyright © 2008
Peter Pauper Press, Inc.
202 Mamaroneck Avenue
White Plains, NY 10601
All rights reserved
ISBN 978-1-59359-492-3
Printed in China
7  6  5  4  3

Visit us at www.peterpauper.com

*Faith is the cornerstone on which all great lives are built.*

*When your mind is full of indecision, try thinking with your heart.*

*The greatest revenge is to accomplish what others say you cannot do.*

*Don't regret what might have been.*
*Accept what is and rejoice in what is yet to be.*

*Don't wait for your world to change.*
*Change it yourself.*

*Live today fully and you create a lifetime of meaningful memories.*

*There are no impossible dreams, just our limited perception of what is possible.*

*It is in the company of a good friend that the heart finds a home.*

*The only true failure is the person who fails to try.*

*You may be disappointed if you fail,*
*but you are certain to be disappointed if you never try.*

*Do great things in your life, but do small things as well.*

*Don't strive to be better than others;*
*strive to be better than your best self.*

*Making life less difficult for others is to be encouraged.*
*Creating happiness for others is to be rewarded.*

*If you measure your value by who you are,*
*there is no end to your reserves.*

*If you can see the beauty of what you aspire to, it doesn't matter if you achieve it all.*
*Simply to aspire is no mean achievement.*

*The past was. Tomorrow may be. Only today is.*

*Don't be frustrated by your inexperience—all green things inevitably grow.*

*The answers will come if you're there to greet them.*

*If the future seems overwhelming,*
*remember that it comes one moment at a time.*

*Self-acceptance gives you the much-needed energy and freedom to grow.*

*Let your dreams be your North Star.*

*You don't need a loud voice to be heard.*
*All you need is something worthwhile to say.*

*If at first you don't succeed—try setting more realistic goals.*

*Be like the birds—sing after every storm.*

*Patience is a skill, perseverance an art.*

*Taking charge of your life takes time—and a bit of faith and courage.*